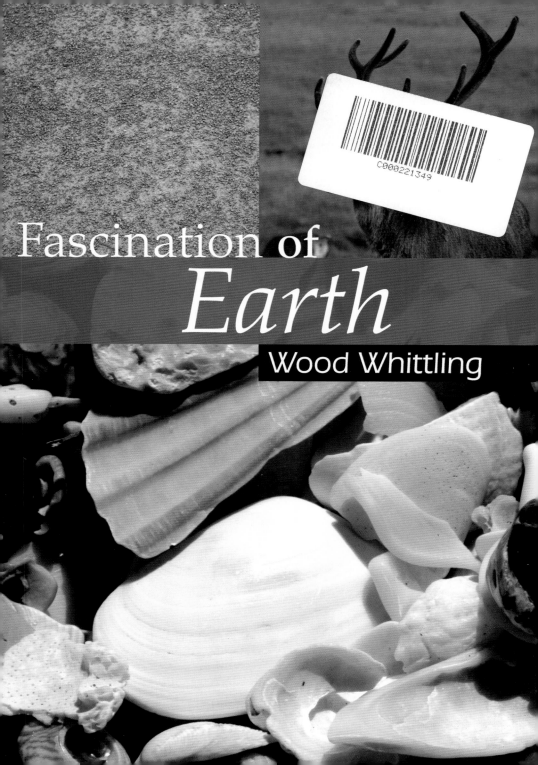

Fascination of *Earth*

Wood Whittling

Many thanks to Dan Phillips, Kate Hookham, Steven White and Petra Babikova, for their contribution and in making this book possible.

Special thanks go to all the children for whom we are in contact with on a daily basis for their joy and inspiration.

© Claire Warden 2011
First published 2012
Reprinted 2015

Design and layout by Almond www.almondtds.com +44 (0)131 553 5523

Printed by J. Thomson Colour Printers, Glasgow, UK

Photography by Claire Warden and the Kindergarten teams.

All photographs © Mindstretchers Ltd

ISBN 978-1-906116-12-5

If you would like training materials or further information about the Fascination series, or any other Mindstretchers publication please contact:
enquiries@mindstretchers.co.uk

Mindstretchers™
The Old School
Fowlis Wester
Crieff
PH7 3NG
Scotland, UK
T: +44 (0)1764 650030
E: enquiries@mindstretchers.co.uk
www.mindstretchers.com

Foreword
by Leif Christensen
Senior Lecturer – Outdoor Pedagogy
University College Lillebaelt, Denmark

This little book is a rich mine of educational reflections and practical hints concerning safety, materials and tools. It is the latest example of the pioneering work done by Claire Warden and Mindstretchers to promote outdoor pedagogy in all its forms.

Probably one of the best-known 'whittlers' in Scandinavia is Emil of Lönneberga, the main character in a series of children's novels by Astrid Lindgren (the Swedish author who also wrote the Pippi Longstocking books). Emil has a prodigious knack for getting into trouble. When his boyish pranks misfire, he runs away and locks himself in the toolshed, or, if he doesn't make it on time, is locked in there by his father as a punishment. In fact, though, Emil does not regard this as a punishment, as he spends the time in there carving figures out of pieces of wood - 369 figures in all over the course of time. Emil's activities in the toolshed contribute considerably to his general education, and he is described as a very intelligent, creative and resourceful person.

Such qualities were also possessed by the Viking craftsmen. The work they did was characterised by the Scandinavian word, 'Sløjd' ('Nordic Sloyd'), which is more or less synonymous with the terms 'craft' in English, though with the added idea that a person who was good at 'Sløjd' was also 'crafty' and artful.

These two examples show a strong connection between manual activities and the character traits of those who practise them. There is a Danish saying that can be quoted in this context: "The products of the hand are the footprints of the soul."

So whittling is a very serious matter indeed!

Many people are of course aware that whittling is a very relaxing, multi-sensory activity – but in fact there is much more to the story than this.

The Norwegian educational researcher, Arne Trageton, has shown that children's constructive play for example, working with actual materials such as clay, sand and wood stimulates their social, linguistic and cognitive development. Since I consider the process of whittling, in which various materials are worked on using a tool to be a more developed form of constructive play, I would expect children's social, linguistic and cognitive skills to be even more stimulated by this process.

I am gratified to see that this book situates the activity of whittling within a broader context. When the hands-on experience gained through working with the hands is placed in a cultural-historical perspective and linked to related areas such as sustainability, the result is improved learning and increased motivation.

Contents

Introduction

Children find fascinating moments in every day, things to be fascinated by or in. Csíkszentmihályi (1990), refers to a state of mind which is all encompassing called the point of flow. Children need time to 'be', to process and to consider the world around them, to allow an enquiring mind to follow its own fascinations so that it can reach a deeper connection. In an education system with a focus on curriculum, a group of researchers came together and started to consider a key question.

'How do we deliver a 'curriculum' through children's fascinations, so that it can be used globally as a methodology for teaching and learning irrespective of the age of the child?'

This series of books is the result of that enquiry. They follow the fascinations of children from three to eleven years old, that we have worked with in play based environments and also in more structured school environments over a number of years.

When we consulted adults, they highlighted a number of issues that were barriers to the promotion of outdoor learning. Skill, knowledge and enthusiasm of the adult; observation of learning; identification and implementation of progression steps; coverage of the curriculum concerns surrounding risk. These issues have structured the content of the books. We hope that an enthusiastic mood overtakes the reader when they read the children's voices, wherever they are in the world.

In order to frame the series, we have taken the natural elements as our guide, Fire, Earth, Air and Water. These give us elements that can then be divided into smaller, deeper fascinations such as charcoal, wood, wind and a puddle. These simple, natural materials conceal the fact that they support complex learning that easily overtakes an inter curricula approach to teaching and learning.

C. Warden.

Claire Warden February 2012

1

Chapter 1. What is Whittling?

There is much debate about whether whittling is in fact wood carving, or whether they are two separate things. In general, we might think of wood carvers who use more complex tools such as gouges or chisels, whereas a whittler, may simply use a pocket knife and a small piece of wood to make a creative shape of some kind. Outlining this distinction is perhaps unnecessary at this point, as they both involve the art of working with wood. It is an area that is both large and varied, and very much worth exploring with all groups over a long period of time.

Many of us have heard or even used the term to 'whittle away the hours', but perhaps have not thought about where this term has derived from. When we say to 'whittle away the hours', we make reference to the traditional art of whittling, where a person uses a sharp implement to shave off pieces from a chunk of wood and create a new shape out of it. The time passes as the whittler becomes fully involved in the process. Whittling has always been a fascination for children, I am sure we can all remember at least one child who was ever so keen to get their first Swiss army knife and then carried it around with them everywhere, as they played in the garden, and explored the outside world.

What you can whittle

Popular items for people to make when whittling, generally include cooking implements such as spoons, forks and knives and crockery such as plates and bowls, or representations of animals like birds and fish. One artist, Chris Lubekmann, specialises in whittling the ends of sticks and twigs to create figures, pen tops and animals which can be found in his book, 'The Art of Whittling'. Making spoons and bowls, for example, requires carving out the wood into a convex shape which can appear difficult to begin with, but once experience has been gained in using the curved edges of the knife, this can be achieved with a bit of perseverance. More basic projects that can be achieved with simple whittling skills, for example, those with a Lancashire potato peeler, mainly involve whittling away bark to make breadsticks, picture frames, or sharpening the end of a stick to make a marshmallow stick, mud pencil or a spear.

Working with wood through history

Art and Industry

Whittling, or wood carving has been around since ancient times. Cavemen, for example, would have shaped wood using sharp stones to make tools and weapons, and examples of people working with wood for both decorative and functional aims spans across history. Evidence, for example, of the finely detailed Egyptian wood carving techniques that were used to create hieroglyphics and figures, can be seen today in museums. In Scotland, we have a tradition of standing stones, many Celtic crosses still exist in villages such as Fowlis Wester near Crieff in Perthshire. The use of carving and whittling techniques to create artworks to honour religious icons, or to decorate places of worship, such as, churches and mosques is vast and one can find many examples when visiting such places. Such examples can be found in the work of the famous Swiss artist Tilman Riemenschneider.

From the seventeenth century, wood was used more and more domestically, creating tables, staircases, room panelling and bed posts. The introduction of wood carving machinery, essentially, put an end to the individual craftsmanship of the artist in this area and opened up the beginning of the timber industry that we see today.

Whittling as a past time

The use of whittling as an activity, was very common by soldiers during the American civil war and as a skill. It soon spread throughout the country when soldiers from across the states would meet around the camp fire and share different techniques. At the end of the war these whittling skills were passed on to children, leading to young boys carrying pen knives in their pockets as they explored the great outdoors. This concept was supported by the growth of the Scouting movement in the mid Nineteenth Century, which supported young boys to engage in camp craft activities, such as basic whittling skills.

Wood carving and whittling, is seen by many today as a pastime and indeed in modern times, it is associated very much with the 'folk scene', of getting back to free and traditional ways of living and working, and connecting with the natural environment. It is used by most groups who engage in Forest School in this country, as a core part of the creative skills that can be developed in natural spaces. Beach School areas that have access to driftwood, have created shelters and dens that use the elements to create characters to embellish their spaces.

Whittling tools

In terms of whittling implements, it is recommended in all literature associated with whittling, that you use a sharp knife, with emphasis on the fact that it is sharp! If you have ever tried carving anything, even a loaf of bread with a blunt knife, you will know how important this is. It is often assumed that sharper knives are the ones that put us most at risk, and are the most likely to cause injuries. In fact, when we explore this issue, we will realise that this is a misconception, and that

A boy aged 10 using a folding pen knife brought from home

sharp knives are actually safer. This is usually because if you have a sharp knife, it will actually cut into what you are trying to carve, or cut rather than slipping onto a softer surface such as your skin. People will recommend many different types of knives for carving with. For example, Scandinavian scouting, use fixed blade knives, fold up pen knives, or even Stanley knives. We generally use fixed blade knives that have a small sharp blade at the end, but during woodland sessions, we will often get some of the older children to bring along their own pen knives that they have used at home.

In terms of working with children in schools, however, we generally use Lancashire potato peelers. Although, perhaps seemingly lacking the impact of a pen knife, these implements work exceptionally well for introducing whittling to a group of school children from 3-11 years, and this is generally what teachers reading this book will be looking to do. The short, fixed blade is used as the skill level increases, and the peelers have done their job in teaching some of the procedures that wrap around safe handling.

Safety equipment

When using Lancashire potato peelers, we generally do not make children wear work gloves, but it can work well to suggest the children wear a work glove on the non-tool hand, which they can then use to pick out pieces of bark that get stuck within the peeler blade. For pupils using a sharp carving or pen knife, it is worth considering buying thumb pads which can help avoid any cuts when starting to learn new techniques.

Types of wood

When it comes to choosing a wood for whittling, experts will suggest that softwoods such as pine are particularly good as they are easier to whittle (with a sharp knife of course!). Hardwoods, such as, Sycamore or Hazel, can work well as can Beech and Oak, although the latter can be more challenging to use.

To whittle well you need to understand the nature of the materials you are using. The grain of the wood is a result of the way that the wood grows at different speeds during the year, creating layers known as growth rings. In terms of whittling skills, we talk about the direction of the grain. In very basic terms, it can be summed up as follows:

- Against the grain – this can be hard work and cause the wood to tear
- With the grain – this is easier and allows for a cleaner finish

Ways to whittle

There are different techniques that can be used for whittling. Firstly, there is the forward stroke which is what we generally use with our children, and the technique which best suits the use of a Lancashire peeler. In using this method, the children will always work the tool away from themselves and this works effectively for whittling off bark and sharpening the end of sticks.

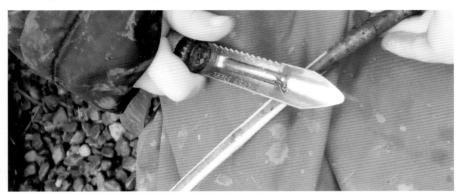

A girl aged three using the straight forward away stroke

Another technique is the draw stroke, whereby the whittler grips the piece of wood firmly, bracing the tool hand with the thumb against the wood. Very precisely, the whittler then cuts towards the body, keeping short and controlled strokes throughout.

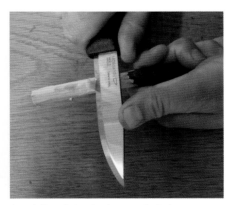

Using a rasp to smooth edges and contour the wood   *An adult participant using a push stroke*

Another common stroke is the push stroke, where the whittler uses the thumb from the other hand to gently push the blade on the knife forward, away from the body. This is again, good for controlled cuts and allows whittlers to make detailed cuts on the wood.

Chapter 2. Case Studies with Analysis and Possible Lines of Development

Case Study 1 – Consulting with children – 3D Mind Map

A group of 2-4 year old children showed an interest in whittling at the nursery. The staff consulted them using the 3D Mind Map with a Talking Tub™ to promote a sharing and exploration of the children's knowledge about wood and whittling. At the beginning of the process, the practitioner put three Lancashire peelers in the middle as a provocation for discussion. The practitioner then opened up the discussion by asking if anyone knew what the tools were used for. One of the children responded by saying, "Peeling potatoes," which then sparked other contributions about peeling fruit and vegetables. When the children spoke their contribution was recorded on the yellow strips of paper and was put down in front of them. When one of the children mentioned peeling trees, small pieces of wood were added to the tools to stimulate discussion about this topic.

As the children explored the objects, their discussion levels increased. When they began talking about peeling the bark, a small bag of bark peelings were introduced for them to explore, "like that," responded one of the children.

When the peelings were shared across the children, they began to explore them and described what they were like with one girl saying,

"It's curly, curly for the nest for the birds."

One of the older boys then commented that,

"They're supposed to protect the trees."

When the session came to an end, several of the children stayed to explore the bark shavings further. One of the young girls began to wrap the bark peelings around one of the sticks, and then used the peelings to make a transient picture, stating that,

"Its a snail."

Following the session, the practitioner arranged all the contributions made by the children into lines of enquiry to help organise the concepts, so that they could be linked to form Possible Lines Of Development (P.L.O.D's). From their contributions, it became clear that the children were particularly interested in exploring the texture and appearance of the bark peelings and were able to link their thinking to knowledge about peeling vegetables.

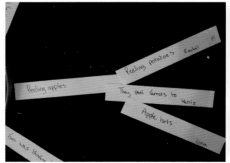

Analysis of learning enabled the children to see their own thinking. The interest and engagement of the children led the team to define the following P.L.O.D's:

- Explore different kinds of bark to focus on texture, appearance and smell
- Offer simple whittling activities, including wood and root vegetables to allow the children to revisit the basic safety procedures when whittling

Case study 2 - Whittling wood (2-6 years)

1. Making Stick People

During an afternoon session in our outdoor area, we found some fallen branches and the children began to explore them. Using their whittling skills, they shaved off the outer bark from the sticks they had found. It was suggested by a member of staff that maybe, they try and make stick men out of the branches.

Two of the older boys took time as they gradually whittled the ends of the branch, and when asked what they were doing, one of them revealed that,

"I am whittling my stick man some hands."

Another of the boys decided to whittle the whole stick saying that he,

"Needs to have smooth skin."

Once they had whittled their sticks, the children used different lengths of wire, string and pine cones to add features to their stick men. One of the young boys used a pine cone as a head, while another wrapped wire around small bracken leaves to make hair on top of the stick man's whittled face.

One of the older boys spent time adding detail to the face of one of the stick men and with some help from the staff, was able to create a detailed face. When he was happy with the face, he used some left over charcoal from the fire to colour in his eyes and mouth.

When the children had created their stick men, they used him in a creative role play scenario. One of the older boys put him up a tree saying that,

"He likes climbing the trees,"

while a small group of children started to create a stick man home using natural materials found in the transient art area. When they had made two different houses, (one from bark and grass and the other from wooden logs), they used the environment as a role play area, giving the stick men names and jobs to do in the home environment.

2. Making pencils

During a morning session outside, the children used their whittling skills to make pencils. Along with a member of staff, they collected fresh branches from a fallen tree and then began to whittle away the ends of their sticks. When asked why she was whittling the sticks, one of the young girls explained that,

> 'It has to be sharp and that's what whittling does."

When asked further why the stick needed to be sharp, the girl responded saying that,

> "It won't work if the pencil isn't sharp, we need it to be pointy."

When the children were happy with their pencils, they used mud ink to write with. They found big pieces of wood and bark to write on.

After testing out the pencils, several of the children went back to the work bench to develop their pencils. One of the girls aged 5 years, used wire to wrap around the pencil to work as a handle. Another of the children, decided to gently whittle the top of the pencil and leave the shavings feathering from the pencil exclaiming that it made it look, "leafy."

They then went back to writing with the pencils with the mud ink. This time, however, the children began to experiment with different surfaces.

They tried out a range of different pieces of wood to see which would work best.

After experimenting on a rounded tree stump, one of the young girls asked for paper and then began writing once more. She spent time trying to write more delicately, so that the lines of her writing were thinner.

She then manipulated the tip of the pencil and pushed back the fibres, so that the pencil remained thin and pointy. When it became too blunt, she intermittently returned to the tool bench and whittled the end until it was sharp again.

One of the boys who had not taken part in the first part of the investigation, came to look at the objects. When he realised that he could write with them, he took the mud ink and pencils inside the kinder kitchen and used them to write in the Floorbook™. When parents arrived, he explained to some of them how the mud ink and pencils worked saying that,

"You just dip it in and write like this, dip, dip, dip."

Several of the parents then signed their names in the Floorbook™, as they collected their children.

Analysis of learning

1. Making stick people

As well as the learning benefits of whittling discussed in Case Study 1, the pupils in this scenario are able to express their creative abilities with wood. One of the boys engages highly, as he finely sculpts the hands and face of his stick man using his pen knife. The use of the pine cone as a head, as well as the entrapment of different natural materials using wire, shows both a high level of manual dexterity and creativity in the design of the stick man features.

The progression to the design and building of the stick man houses, highlights further creativity with the natural materials, and emphasises the value of the stick people as a provocation for role play and storytelling opportunities.

> ## PLODS
>
> 1) Develop creation of stick people stories using the whittled stick men as motivations for storytelling/writing.
>
> 2) Create accessories for the stick man figures and use to stimulate further creative language opportunities linked to role play and small world moments.
>
> 3) Provide opportunities for decorating the candle holders using natural paints, charcoal or calligraphy to encourage creative expression.

2. Making pencils

The children show an understanding of the need for their pencils to be thin in order to write properly with them, which is something they are able to achieve by the use of their whittling skills. When the young girl whittles her stick again, once it has become too soft, it underlines her ability to maintain the dimensions of the pencil. Several of the children are able to express their creativity with their whittling skills, by whittling the tops of the pencil and leaving parts of the peeled bark attached to the wood. The exploration of using mud as an ink shows resourcefulness, and the time spent mixing the mud together, highlights their knowledge of mixing solutions to create suspensions. Several of the children write on different pieces of wood before settling on the use of paper, highlighting a use of experimentation and perseverance with the activity. The application of the whittled pencils for writing with the mud ink, provides an example of ways of engaging the children with literacy, and the success of the children in writing their names highlights this. Parents and carers took these skills and fed back that they had made more 'pencils' at home and made other 'inks.'

PLODS

1) Experiment further with different types of materials for writing with such as, chalk, water, natural paints and charcoal to explore writing skills.

2) Make pencils using different types of wood to determine the differences between soft and hardwoods and different species of tree.

Case Study 3 – Whittling wood (7-8 years)

1. Making measuring sticks

During an outdoor learning session in the local woodland, the school class explored their current interest in number and measurement. The class already had several woodland sessions, where they had learned the skills for sawing and whittling safely. The class were given pieces of fresh wood and access to a variety of tools in order to create a measuring stick. The pupils began by whittling their stick using a potato peeler.

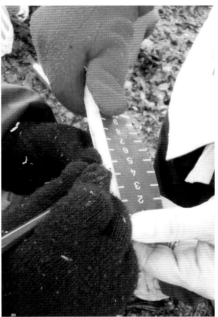

When the children had whittled all of the bark from their stick, they used a measuring tape to determine where they should mark out the measurements on their own stick. It was decided to use centimetres as the unit of measurement on the stick. Several of the children used a pencil to mark on the whittled wood, while others used paint pens. During a discussion about this, one of the children commented that, "I'm going to use pencil, "Cos it won't rub off." The children experimented with different ways of marking accurately, some worked with a partner who held the measuring tape in place, while others put both the measuring tape and stick on the ground and matched them up.

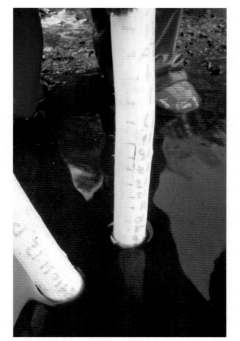

When they had finished marking the numbers, the children marked their initials on the bottom of the stick and laid them out to dry on the ground.

Due to so much rainy weather over the past few days, it was suggested that the children use their new measuring sticks to measure the different depths of the many puddles on the path. The children first estimated how deep they were and then used their sticks to work out the depth.

2. Making Photo Frames

During a session in the woods, the class used their whittling skills to make a photo frame. As part of the management plan for the wood, it was decided to bring in a selection of fresh wood harvested in advance by the session leader. The pupils found appropriate areas to begin their whittling activity, some sat on the floor, others on logs, while some sat in the hammocks. When asked about whittling, one of the pupils described that,

"I really liked doing the whittling because you get a knife and scrape all the wood off. It lets you think about all sorts. You can make it smooth if you work hard,"

while another commented that,

"I like it because it's easy to do but you get good looking results that you can be proud of."

When the sticks had been whittled, the children sawed the stick into four pieces. They used a measuring tape, or their own wooden measure, so that all the sticks were the right length to fit the shape that they wanted to create.

Any missed pieces of bark, were then whittled from the individual sticks and any designs were made into the wood. When questioned about the whittling process, one of the pupils described that, "You have to push the peeler down the stick. It's green under the bark, but if you keep going it turns white." When the pupils were happy that there sticks had been whittled enough, they arranged the pieces on the woodland floor. Some pupils created squares and rectangles, while others made triangles.

String was then used to tie the pieces together. Pupils used a square lash to ensure that the sticks were connected tightly.

When the frames had been fixed together, the pupils created transient art inside them using the woodland materials. A group of children experimented with artworks using the frames together to make a range of sculptural forms.

Analysis of learning

This experience of whittling in itself provides a variety of learning benefits. In each scenario, the pupils are able to explore the properties of wood as they gently peel the layers of bark back, and feel the existence of sap that creates the soft, almost buttery feel to the wood. In scenario one, for example, several pupils spent up to thirty minutes whittling their pieces of wood, showing a particular high level of engagement and apparent similar level of well being. Moreover, the practical application of the pupil's awareness of risk is important, as we can see that the pupils have learned how to correctly whittle in order to keep themselves and others safe. This is surmised, when one of the pupils describes back in class that, "Whittling is a skill that needed great concentration in case you cut anyone by accident."

Bringing the very practical activity of whittling, together with the use of number and measurement allows mathematical understanding to be applied within a context, which can often help to make the learning more motivational for pupils. This concept, is applied in a similar way through the photo frame making, as the pupils then progress from whittling the wood to measuring the wood appropriately to explore shape and size. The creation of both the measuring sticks and frames provide the opportunity to explore an area of the curriculum in focus; the pupils progress to measuring the depth of the puddles on the estate road using the measuring sticks, and the pupils progress to creating natural art inside the frames. The progression of learning here is key, as we see the pupils apply their whittling skills to gain a greater depth and application.

PLODS for measuring sticks:

1) Experiment with different ways to mark wood such as marker pens, pencils, paint, charcoal and pyrography and choose which tool is the most effective.

2) Investigate the different layers of bark on trees, focusing on the differences between inner and outer bark and what both trees and people use them for.

3) Provide further opportunities for measuring natural elements, such as puddles in the local environment. Support pupils to collect and record their results and interpret them appropriately.

PLODS for making frames:

1) Explore different ways for decorating frames using paints, natural materials or markings.

2) Research ways to preserve wood and provide the opportunity for pupil experimentation with methods of preservation.

3) Introduce other types of knots which can be used when working with wood such as, whipping.

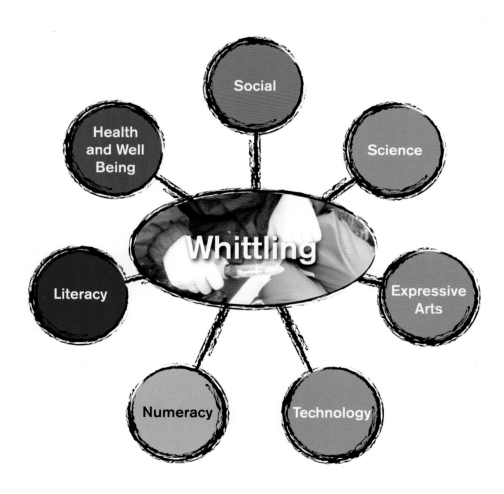

Area of enquiry

1. Knowledge of types of wood and bark
2. Different materials for wood marking

Area of enquiry

1. Creation of artefacts (Case study 1 & 2)
2. Use of wood and bark shavings for creativity

Area of enquiry

1. Design and creation of equipment/implements (Case study 1)
2. Development of technology in whittling use
3. Methods for preserving wood

Area of enquiry

1. Promoting mathematical concepts such as measurement, shape and time (Case study 1)

Area of enquiry

1. Whittling as a tool for creating writing implements (Case study 1 & 2)
2. Opportunities for functional/anecdotal writing

Area of enquiry

1. Children's awareness and management of risk (Case study 1 & 2)
2. Active outdoor learning experiences (Case study 1 & 2)
3. Whittling as an activity to promote well being and concentration (Case study 1 & 2)
4. Use of whittling skills in food preparation

Area of enquiry

1. Historical use of whittling as a skill
2. Natural resources in the environment (Case study 2)

Area of enquiry concept/knowledge/skill	Opportunities for experiential learning experiences
1. Conceptual knowledge of types of wood and bark	
When wood is freshly cut it is easy to bend because it contains water (sap). This also makes whittling bark very easy as it comes straight off.	Provide pupils with a selection of freshly cut green branches and dead sticks and encourage them to try bending or breaking them and explore the different properties of each. This can be used as a starting point to discuss why sticks have such different characteristics.
Certain trees such as Oak and Beech are called hardwoods, whereas trees such as, Pine and Larch are considered softwood. Hardwood has a more complex structure and is generally harder to work with than softwoods.	Cut some small pine and oak branches and allow pupils to whittle them to see if they can notice any differences when working with the wood. This experience could then form the basis for a research investigation into soft and hardwoods.
2. Different materials for wood marking	
You can effectively mark and draw on wood using pens, lead pencils, charcoal and some natural paints.	Support pupils to whittle the bark from a fresh and then encourage them to decorate or mark using a material or solution of their choosing. Offer pupils a range of materials that can be used for marking and investigate which one works the best.
Pyrography is a traditional method that uses heat to mark wood.	Research the traditional method of pyrography and look at the range of different artworks and pieces that have been created using this technique.

Expressive Arts	Area of enquiry concept/knowledge/skill	Opportunities for experiential learning experiences
1. Creation of artefacts		
		Allow the children freedom to use their whittling skills to produce a range of creative artefacts from whittling the bark of a stick to make it look like a tree, to delicately shaping the end of a stick into a bird shape. A range of additional resources such as string, wire, leaves, bark could be used to develop their ideas.
2. Exploration of wood and bark shavings		
	The shavings of wood and bark can be used as a resource for a wide range of different purposes.	Once the children have whittled, encourage them to be as creative as they can with the bark shavings and to see what they can make. The bark can work excellently as hair or clothes for small world scenarios.
	Wood and bark shaving provide a rich sensorial material to explore smell, texture and appearance.	Work with the children to explore wood shavings as material and encourage them to describe their different experiences with it. Due to its range of sensorial properties, this will provide a rich stimulation for language.

Area of enquiry concept/knowledge/skill	Opportunities for experiential learning experiences
1. Design and creation of different equipment/utensils	
Implements such as rulers, frames, cutlery and cooking sticks can be made using simple whittling techniques.	Support the children to make their own utensils using their whittling skills. The children could be shown pictures of wooden spoons, forks, knives, picture frames, rulers and stirrers and be supported to make this.
2. Development of technology in whittling and carving	
	Children can be given the opportunity to research the ways that people throughout history have used machines and resources to produce charcoal. Small rates of production using a small kiln can be compared to mass production in industry.
3. Methods for preserving wood	
A range of different solutions such as olive, walnut, linseed and vegetable oil can be used to help preserve wood once it has been whittled.	Provide the children with a range of different oils and conduct an experiment to determine which ones preserve the wood the most effectively. The focus could be on colour, smell, texture and appearance.

Area of enquiry concept/knowledge/skill	Opportunities for experiential learning experiences
1. Recording mathematical thinking	
The use of whittled pens and homemade inks can be used to help motivate children to engage with maths.	Support the children to use their homemade inks and whittled pens to record their mathematical thinking on a range of different surfaces in both the indoor and outdoor environment.
2. Promoting mathematical concepts such as measurement, shape and time	
	Encourage the children to design the artefacts and utensils that they will make using the whittling skills, ensuring that they focus on detailing measurements and exact recordings of their ideas. During the process of making the utensils, encourage the children to use their mathematical skills to measure out the wood and to think about the shapes involved in making their product.

Area of enquiry concept/knowledge/skill	Opportunities for experiential learning experiences
1. Whittling as a tool for making writing implements	
	Whittling skills can be used to sharpen the ends of wood which can then be used as pencils or pens for dipping in different kinds of inks and solutions.
	These pens can then be experimented with on a range of different surfaces such as paper, wood and different materials.
2. Opportunities for functional and anecdotal writing	
	The process of whittling can be a motivating stimulus for creating functional writing for example, pupils can be supported to write Safety procedures or 'How to Guides.' Pupils could also be supported to use the experience of whittling for anecdotal writing, such as poetry about why they like whittling.

Area of enquiry concept/knowledge/skill	Opportunities for experiential learning experiences
1. Children's awareness and management of risk	
Children are able to self risk assess and the more we can trust them to make decisions and provide supportive environments for them to do so, the more they will thrive.	Children can be supported to create their own Benefit Risk Assessment about whittling. This will encourage them to make decisions about how to look after themselves and others. This risk assessment can be written down by children, or recorded from their words by an adult.
2. Active outdoor learning experiences	
Whittling is an activity that is very appropriate for taking outside.	Children can be encouraged to explore the outdoor area and look for wood that might be suitable for whittling. If there are no trees in the area, they could be given the task of searching for trees in their garden or local park, and finding out if they would be suitable for whittling.
3. Whittling as an activity to promote well being and concentration	
Whittling is considered by many people as an activity that is therapeutic.	Organise a whittling activity where the children are given a sense of space and freedom so that they can have the opportunity to engage fully with their whittling activity. Ensuring that correct supervision and safety coaching has taken place prior to this activity, will ensure that the activity is relatively low risk. When doing this activity, encourage the teacher to step back and observe the engagement and well being levels of the children.
4. Use of whittling skills in food preparation	
The same whittling technique when using Lancashire peelers can be used for peeling fruit and vegetables.	Encourage children to use their whittling skills to help peel fruit and vegetables which could be eaten for snack or lunch.

Area of enquiry concept/knowledge/skill	Opportunities for experiential learning experiences
1. Historic use of whittling as a skill	
Whittling and wood carving has been used by a variety of different people and communities throughout history in the areas of art, religion, industry and recreation.	Set the children a research task to find out as much as they can about whittling and woodcarving on the internet. They will find different examples from country folk whittling spoons and bowls, to wood sculptures in cathedrals.
2. Natural resources in the environment	
Wood can be a sustainable energy resource if it is used sensibly and we plant and look after the trees in the environment.	Research why using wood in sensible quantities can make it a sustainable resource. The children could find out about deforestation and aforestation.
Softwoods are the main source of wood used for timber products.	The use of wood as a resource could start a tree planting project, or a conservation activity within the school, which could help raise the children's contribution to their local school environment and allow them to make a contribution to future generations.

Chapter 4. Developing Skills

How to run a whittling session

Why whittling?

We see whittling as an activity that allows children freedom, flexibility and a chance for a lot of personal space to connect with their sense of self and their natural environment. Whittling is an activity that we use on a regular basis in our Nature Kindergartens, during our work with teachers and as part of our project work with our Living Classrooms Charity. When we introduce whittling to a group, whether it be a small group of three year olds, or a group of adults, we find that the engagement and wellbeing levels of the individuals generally increase and that the sensibility to both the environment and peers increases.

We have conducted whittling sessions where we have started the children off and simply stepped back and allowed it to continue for an hour, or even more. Sometimes, the child may use their whittling skills to make a cooking stick, or a photo frame or perhaps even a weapon. Sometimes, it might just be whittling for whittling's sake as they explore the feel of shaving away the rough bark from the smooth sap wood and concentrate so much on what they are doing, that the rest of the world almost stops around them. It is this type of deep level engagement that we strive for everyday in education. We are not saying that whittling will always create this, but it is absolutely an activity that can create high engagement and fascinate children and therefore, in our opinion, should be made available to children of all ages within the learning environment at school.

Where to start

When working with children in an educational environment, you will start off by whittling the bark from pieces of wood. The focus in this respect, would be to ensure that the wood that the children are whittling is reasonably fresh, so that they can easily shave the bark from the wood itself. Before you start with the children, it is well worth practicing yourself on a small fresh piece of wood and then an old dead bit of wood to see the difference. As you begin to integrate whittling into your practice, you will find that ensuring that the children are whittling fresh wood will help with safety, as they will have more success and will not start to experiment with different techniques to get the bark away, which can often be unsafe. Another aspect to consider is the knots in wood. The knots that we find in wood are old branches that have snapped off and then slowly inverted into the wood. When children are whittling with peelers, you will find that they will struggle when they try and whittle over a knot, or when they try to shave off a knot. The best thing to do here, would be to either let a staff member cut it off, or encourage the children to whittle around the knot.

Transference of skill – kitchen to whittling

Group management

Whether we are working out in the woods, in the playground or in the classroom, we will always designate a tool area, whereby, anyone wishing to whittle, for example, has to stay. This allows a staff member to keep an eye on the children with the tools.

Where to sit

It is also important to establish appropriate seating or kneeling room for children. A log or low bench works well as it allows children to straighten out their legs and whittle to the side of them. If there is no appropriate seating, then children are normally made to sit on one knee and whittle away to the ground. There is never an occasion where a child is allowed to whittle sitting down on their bottom, on the floor, as this can open up the possibility of a child cutting their leg.

Ensuring safety

When working with children, or indeed adults of any age, we use the concept of a 'blood bubble' to help support the children to keep themselves and one another safe. The 'blood bubble', is a safe area around a child that no other person is allowed to walk in, meaning that they can use their tool without fear of cutting anyone else. The 'blood bubble', is measured by the child reaching out all the way around themselves and ensuring that he cannot touch anyone.

A girl aged six struggling to whittle the bark from the dead wood

What to use

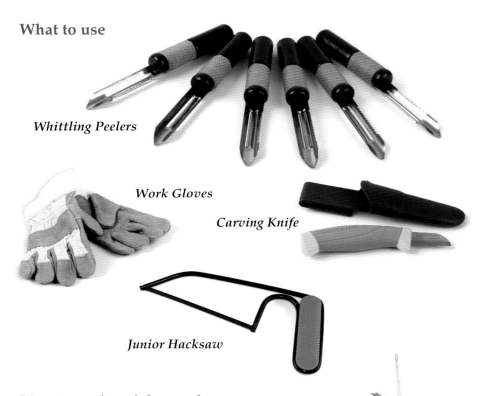

Whittling Peelers

Work Gloves

Carving Knife

Junior Hacksaw

How to make stick people

The joy of making stick people is to search the forest for branches and twigs that already have the hint of arms and legs coming from it.

1. Use the whittling tool of choice to shape the ends of the arms and legs. Peel off the bark to create feet and hand areas. Some people carve stripes and shapes into the 'body' for clothing.

2. Run the blade around the 'neck' of the person to create a line and whittle the head shape with facial features and a neck area.

3. Use charcoal to enhance the facial features.

4. Make a hole in the top to add hair made from loose materials such as shavings or twigs.

How to make a spoon

Birch and Sycamore are easier woods to begin with. You will need the following:

- Straight knife
- Carving knife
- Mallet
- Sandpaper
- Oil (food grade)

1. Select a small pole about 6cm in diameter that is green and therefore, softer to work with. Try and find one with a natural curve, or slight 'dog leg' that you can use as the curve of the spoon.

2. Start by cutting the pole to a little longer than you need for the finished spoon and split the pole in half, lengthways. To do this, place your knife with the edge across one end of the pole and carefully, using an off cut from your pole as a mallet, knock your knife into the pole. Allow it to split slowly, as forcing it at this stage may make the split run off centre. Select the half that is shaped in the right way for the spoon you want to carve and whittle the split surface with your knife so that it is smooth.

3. Using a pencil, roughly draw a spoon shape on to the wood, you could use any spoon which you like the shape of as a template for this. Using the knife carefully, whittle and slice around the outline until you have completed shaping in that plane. The grain in the wood may run in different directions and dictate which way you can cut.

4. Look at your spoon from the side and decide how you would like to shape the curve of the spoon handle. If you have managed to use a pole with a natural curve or dog-leg it may only need a little refining. Always use your knife carefully, making sure that you are always cutting away from yourself. If you have made the handle of your spoon wide in one plane, you can make it thin in the other plane and vice versa, shaping in this way will ensure that the spoon remains strong enough.

5. When you are satisfied with the shape of your spoon, you can turn your attention to shaping the inside of the bowl. With your hooked knife, slowly start to remove all the unwanted wood, the grain of the wood will dictate which direction you will need to cut in but in general, cutting across the grain works well. When this is finished, you can start finishing the spoon.

6. If you intend to sand the spoon to a smooth finish, store it at room temperature for a few days first, this will dry the wood out a little and make sanding easier. If you intend leaving your spoon with a tooled finish, carefully go over the spoon with your knife, fine-tuning any slightly rough or uneven areas.

7. Finally, seal your spoon with oil, a person once said that a wooden spoon allows you to taste every meal you have ever eaten with it, as a hint stays within the wood. The food grade oils will bring out the markings in the wood and also be safe for eating with.

Chapter 5. Benefit Risk Assessment

Benefit Risk Assessment	Fire based activities
Assessment date: 06/2011	Date for review: 09/2011 - ongoing
Assessment undertaken by:	Staff member
Approved by:	Senior staff member
Local site Considerations/amendments:	Unstable tree branches, low level branches, overhang area of trees. Uneven ground conditions, or obstacles on the ground. Wood is collected from sustainable areas and done effectively without harming the tree/bush. Weather effects on ground, seating areas and other surfaces.
Benefits of whittling/ wood carving:	• Opportunity for children to self-risk assess • Build self confidence • Group co-operation • Group awareness • Build independence and develop trust • Understanding the use of tools - creative and functional • Build fine motor skills • Develop woodcarving skills • Develop an understanding of the properties of wood • Calming and therapeutic aspects of whittling

Hazard	Level of risk	Precaution	Revised risk level
Medical conditions - respiratory issues	Medium	• Allergies and medical Low respiratory issues conditions/ requirements are checked prior to activity • Participants manage their own medication or managed by supervising adult (age appropriate)	Low
Inappropriate behaviour during wood carving/ whittling activity	High	• Staff have received training in working with vulnerable groups/ are Disclosure Scotland checked • Adult ratio is appropriate and adult is positioned appropriately to monitor children's whittling techniques and safety procedures • Adult ratio is appropriate for supervising rest of group if near designated whittling activity area • All pupils are instructed to move and behave appropriately and with care around tool areas e.g. use of blood bubble • Appropriate personal protective equipment is available and worn by participants • Zero tolerance to inappropriate use of tools. If occurs, tools are immediately removed from pupil and time out from activity is given	Low

Hazard	Level of risk	Precaution	Revised risk level
Contact with sharp implements	High	• Gloves for adults and children are available to protect hands during tool use. Gloves are worn on the non tool hand • Pupils are trained in the use of tools and given demonstrations and training • Tools are introduced progressively to pupils. Start with Lancashire peeler and move up to pen knife/fixed blade knife only when appropriate • Adults have valid first aid qualifications • Fresh wood is always used to begin with as it is easier to whittle • Pupils are encouraged to whittle around knots in wood or adult removes knots with a knife before or during session	Low

Hazard	Level of risk	Precaution	Revised risk level
Inappropriate use of tools	High	• Adults are trained and aware of appropriate tool handling techniques • Wood used is selected to be appropriate to activity. Eg. Willow for charcoal, Larch/Spruce to bend, Hazel to strip, Elder to create necklaces • Teach children how to use tools and equipment correctly and using appropriate personal protective equipment • Children are monitored and supported if necessary when carrying materials. Safe carrying and storing strategies are taught for all tools • Creation of a whittling zone with designated seating/storage area • Whittling - used in a seated position, drawing the knife/peeler away from the body and legs, potato peelers available on forest wrap. Adult knife stored in adult hip belt and managed on a higher ratio • All tools are monitored, treated and stored appropriately at end of the activity	Low
Cuts or injuries - from wood handling, from hazardous plants and from tool handling	Medium	• Adults have appropriate first aid training. First aid point established. First aid kit monitored and replenished daily as appropriate • Cuts or injuries from wood/tool handling are cleaned and treated immediately and first aid requirements dealt with appropriately • Children are monitored and supported, if necessary when carrying materials. Safe lifting strategies are taught • Hazardous plants/locations must be identified in advance and contact with them prevented if appropriate	Low

Summary

The journey through this book has explored the connection of children to the fascination of wood whittling. The process of changing a piece of nature into a new form with a new purpose, that may range from functional tool making, to the creative process of patterning and reforming to accentuate the beauty of a piece. Children around the world are being given the opportunities to re-connect to nature through following a variety of routes. Traditional crafts and skills are part of our intergenerational knowledge. These traditions hold us together as a culture, they acknowledge our ancestors in a living, practical way. Children show us in their play that the mastery of these skills fascinate them, the transformational process engages all aspects of their being.

This book has been created to support adults to see the benefits of working with the natural elements as a way of teaching and learning. The inclusion of curriculum concepts and skills lead to longer term developments in attitude, that stay with the learner throughout their lives. We need to be able to identify and document learning outside, to reinforce links across three learning environments of inside, outside and beyond, if we are to support children, families and educational groups to 'be' outside in nature.

If you are enjoying this book, I would suggest you explore the other titles in the series that are, Fire, Earth, Water and Air.

With kind regards

C. Warden.

Do keep in touch through **www.claire-warden.com**
or through the publishers **www.mindstretchers.com**

Mindstretchers Publications

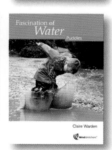

A new series of books that provide an insight into the knowledge you need as an adult to facilitate learning occurring in outdoor environments. Includes case studies with analysis and Possible Lines of Development (P.L.O.D) with full colour photography throughout.

'The true value of this little gem of a book is that it respects the power of allowing children to have their own adventures, follow their own imaginations and make their own discoveries.' Tim Gill

'An invaluable and inspirational resource, by an internationally recognized expert in her field, that beautifully illustrates the power of nature to amplify every dimension of learning.' Richard Louv

Available in 2012, a series of 4 Fascinations: Fire; Earth; Water; Air.

Price £9 each (A5 paperback)

E-book version available (EPUB and Kindle)

visit www.mindstretchers.com for worldwide online retail outlets

To find out more about all of Claire Warden's books visit **www.claire-warden.com** or go to **www.mindstretchers.com** to order online

Published by
Mindstretchers™

Email enquiries@mindstretchers.co.uk
Tel +44(0)1764 650030

Inspirational Learning, Inside, Outside and Beyond